Emmi Lou Noor

A CRICKED
NAMED BRUNO

My Favorite Corona Tale

Produced and published by BoD – BOOKS on DEMAND,
Norderstedt
www.bod.de
Printed and bound in Germany
ISBN: 978-3-7519-5515-7

For Stine

Based on a True Story

It was the time when just about everything changed for us from one day to the next. My school closed and so did the day care of my little brother Max. We had to stay at home most of the time and we couldn't even go to the playground anymore. Because it was also closed. The swimming pool, the cinema and the ice cream shop around the corner were closed. And even the restaurant across the street where they had the most delicious pizza in the world. We couldn't go shopping for clothes anymore and no shoes either. And I was really looking forward to my new sandals.

Mom stopped going to work. She had to take care of us because Grandma and Grandpa weren't allowed to visit us anymore. Mom said, it was because of a new cough for which there was no cough syrup yet. And because no planes were flying anymore, Dad couldn't come home either. He was in New Zealand at the time.

We were very sad about everything. Most of all Max. "Daddy! I want Daddy!" he whimpered at night as we lay in bed.
"Daddy's coming soon. I'm sure he will!" I said. But Max pulled the blanket over his head and kept on whimpering. I sighed and was wondering how I could comfort him, when all of a sudden I heard a faint sound. What was that? I sat up and listened. It sounded like... yes, it sounded like a chirping! Like the chirping of a grasshopper!

I turned on my night table lamp and looked around. Where was the chirping coming from? Finding out wasn't so easy. So I got up and tiptoed around our room with my ears pricked up.

"What are you doing?" asked Max who was looking out curiously from under the blanket.

"Shhh, do you hear that chirping!?" I whispered.
Listening, Max's eyes widened. Then he nodded.
"It has to be a grasshopper. Maybe he flew in from outside."
Max looked to the window and thought hard.
"Remember last summer? In Grandma and Grandpa's garden? When we caught grasshoppers in the meadow?"
I took a picture off the bulletin board and gave it to Max.
It was a picture of a grasshopper crawling over my finger.

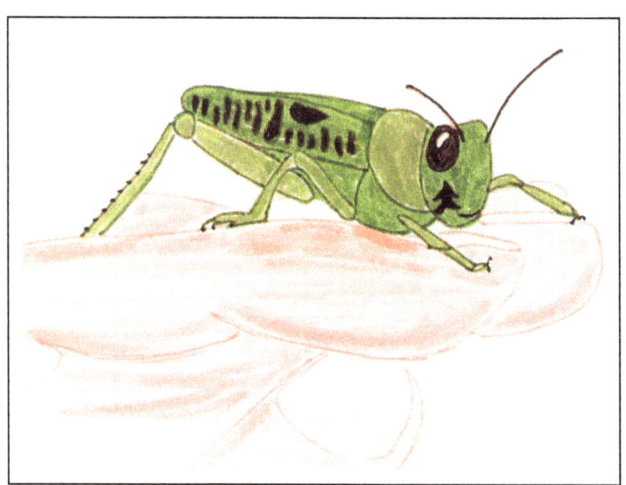

Max looked at the picture. Then he said:
"Yes, grasshopper!"
It was as if his tears had been blown away.

"Where is he?" Max wanted to know.

"I don't know," I said. "But if you help me look, we can open the window and set him free."

Max got out of bed and we looked around on the floor together. We looked behind the trash, shook the heavy curtains and looked in all the corners. We peeked behind my desk, and used the flashlight to light up the crack between bed and wall. Max even looked under Grandpa's old wardrobe.

But the grasshopper was nowhere to be found.

"I'm cold," Max said.

"Me too," I said. "Let's look again tomorrow, ok?"

"Ok," Max said and got back into his bed. Then he asked: "Annabelle?"

"Yes?"

"Are you coming to snuggle?"

And when I saw how he was looking at me with his big, brown eyes and chattering teeth, I turned off the light and crawled to Max under the blanket. There I snuggled up against him.

"Max?" I said after we'd been lying together for a while and feeling warmer.

"Yes?"

"Are you excited about being back with Grandma and Grandpa again?"

"Yes!"

"I'm looking forward to the swing."

"Me too."

"And maybe Grandma will bake apple strudel for us!"

"Yes! With vanilla ice cream!"

"Yum!"

And as I imagined all this, I was already asleep the next moment.

When Max and I woke up the next morning, the chirping was still there. Right after breakfast, we started looking again. But the grasshopper was nowhere to be found. Max lost interest and wanted to play now.

I went into the living room: "Mom?"

"Yes?"

"May I use your computer?"

"What for?"

"We have a grasshopper in our room."

"This time of year?"

"Yes! And now I have to look up how to catch him. We want to set him free outside."

Mom was still looking at me skeptically.

"Come with me, if you don't believe me and listen for yourself," I shouted.

When Mom and I entered our room, Max was sitting on the floor. He had his Lego spread out all over the floor, even in my half of the room. But today I didn't care.

"Do hear?" I asked, and saw Mom listening.

"I do," she said after a while and looked around.

"We've already looked everywhere. But we can't find him," I said, and Max nodded as if to confirm. "But maybe we can lure him into a trap."

Mom even took a look up at the ceiling. Then she looked at me smiling: "Well, I just have to turn on the computer for you then."

"Yes!" I called and ran back to the living room. Max ran after me.

Mom turned on her computer and Max climbed onto my lap. Fascinated, he looked at the screen, at the pictures of different grasshoppers. I even found a sound recording. But the chirping that could now be heard sounded completely different.

"We don't have a grasshopper," I said, amazed and also a little disappointed.

"What then?" asked Mom.

I didn't have a clue! So we listened to the chirping of various insects: cicada, locust... But they also sounded completely different. At the next chirping, Max shouted excitedly: "Yes, that! That's the one!!!"

He was right. The chirping we heard now sounded almost exactly like the chirping in our room.

"And what is it?" Mom asked curiously.

"It's an a-che-ta do-mes-ti-cus," I deciphered.

"A what?" Mom asked laughing.

"Acheta domesticus," I repeated and we all really had to laugh.

"It's Latin. Acheta means 'singer'. 'Domesticus' means 'home.' We have a 'home singer'. But it's also called a cricket."

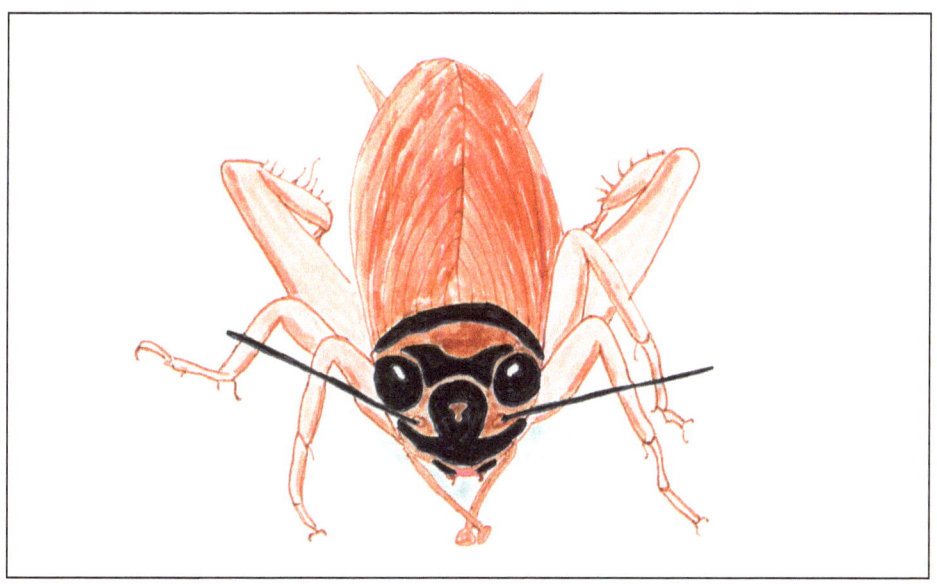

"So, you two are already my home singers," Mom said.

"Yes, because we're always home!" Max said, and we laughed even more.

Once we settled down again, I read on: "The chirping is made by males that are ready to mate when they rub their front wings. They attract the females in this way."

Max giggled.

"So, you have a male," Mom said.

"Yes! We could give him a name!?"

"Bruno!" cried Max promptly and his eyes lit up.

"Ok!" I said. "A cricket named Bruno!"

Max slipped off my lap, climbed onto the sofa, and jumped and hopped around: "Bruno, Bruno, Bruno!" until Mom shooed us into our room. There we built a spaceship for Bruno so that he could soon fly home again.

We had been playing for a while when I noticed that Bruno had stopped chirping. He was probably tired and resting for the night. Dad's nature guide said crickets are nocturnal and afraid of the light. The females look particularly frightening at first sight because they have a huge stinger. But this is only the ovipositor. They use it to lay their eggs in the ground.

We also found out that crickets are a popular food insect for geckos, turtles, lizards and birds. And in many parts of the world people even eat crickets and locusts.

Ugh!

After dinner we built a trap for Bruno. We filled an empty glass with lettuce, carrots and oatmeal to lure Bruno into it. Then we placed the trap on the floor just below our window.

We couldn't fall asleep for a long time. We were so excited. Again and again we kept turning on the light, checking to see if Bruno had already fallen into the trap. But at some point, our eyes closed.

"Good night, Bruno!" I said and yawned.

"Good night, Bruno!" Max said and yawned, too. Then it was quiet. It was only Bruno chirping in the darkness.

The next morning we checked the trap right away. But the trap was empty and the food untouched. To be honest I was quite happy, because in this way we could keep Bruno a little longer.

From now on Mom was not allowed to use the vacuum cleaner in our room anymore – because of Bruno! And Max invented a funny game: When we moved through the room, we were only allowed to touch the floor as little as possible to avoid accidentally trampling Bruno.

That's why when Max had to go to the toilet at night, he would call my name and throw stuffed animals at me until I woke up and turned on the light. Only then did he carefully set foot on the floor.

The next few days we watched a lot of cricket videos and even wrote a song for Bruno! It went like this:

"Hear, one night | children cried
tiny Bruno came, alright
chirped there | anywhere
Bruno didn't care
So the kids, they searched around
looking for the lovely sound
night and day | please oh stay
Bruno come and play"

And then Daddy came home! I was doing schoolwork when he suddenly walked in the door. Mom hadn't told us anything to surprise us. I was so happy that he was home again. I wanted to be in his arms all day long.

To celebrate the day, we decided that we would have Spaghetti Bolognese – our favorite food. Mom, Max and I immediately went to the supermarket to buy everything. Dad had to stay home because of the quarantine. But he wanted to unpack first anyway and arrive in peace.

But when we came back, Dad was in our room. He was standing on the ladder with a screwdriver in his hand. He was working on the white round thing on the ceiling.

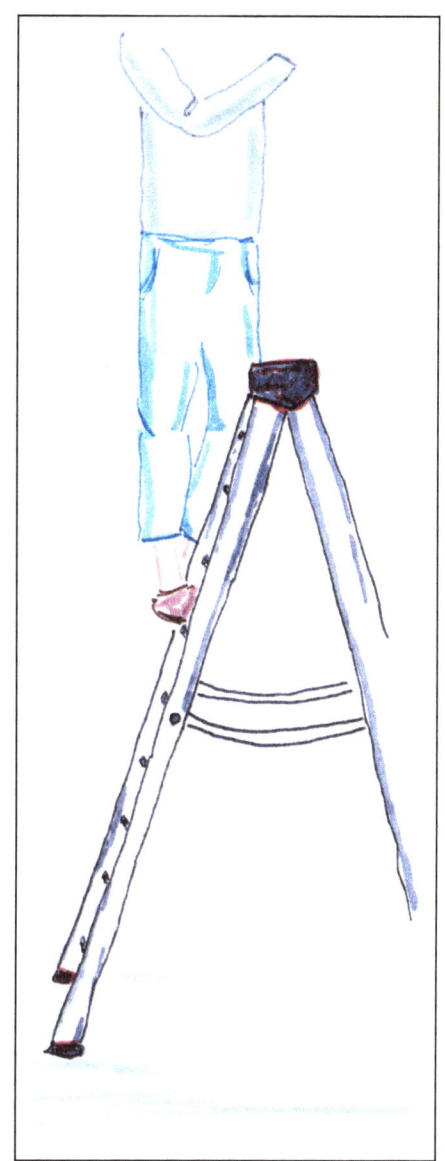

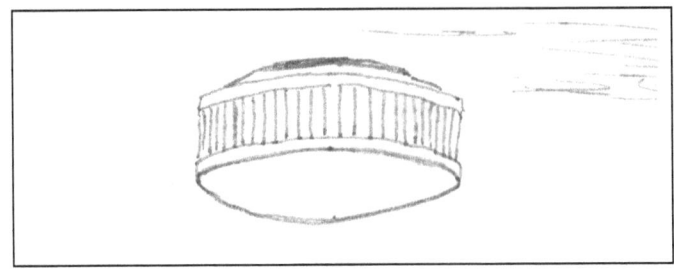

"What are you doing?" I asked in surprise.

"I just want to change the smoke detector battery," Dad said. "Don't you hear that annoying chirping?"

"But... but that's Bruno!" protested Max.

"Yes, Bruno! Our cricket!" I agreed with him. "He got lost in our room and now he lives..."

I couldn't speak anymore because at that moment Dad opened the cover of the smoke detector. The chirping was now clearly audible. We held our breath. Papa took out the battery – the chirping stopped. Max looked terrified and made no sound. I was shocked too. I took a few steps and looked up at the smoke detector.

Then I said: "Bruno's dead!"

Max started to cry bitterly. But I looked at Mom and remembered how she had stood in our room and looked at the ceiling. Now everything became clear to me.

"You knew it!" I shouted outraged.

She nodded.

"You knew it all this time and didn't tell us?!" I just couldn't believe it.

"This hasn't been an easy time for any of us," Mom said. "And I thought it would be nice for you to have a new friend. Even though he's invisible."

Although we were happy that Daddy was back home, we were very sad. We had lost Bruno and we missed him very much. Max wasn't even hungry for Spaghetti Bolognese that evening. And that's saying something.

Without Bruno we realized again how dumb it was that we couldn't go out and meet our friends whenever we wanted. And the most beautiful spring sunshine you could imagine was shining outside.

It was soon Easter. We were playing in our room when Mom and Dad suddenly called out: "Max! Annabelle! Come quickly, the Easter Bunny was here there!"

We raced out, but as soon as we entered the living room, we stopped in surprise because we heard a loud chirping sound!

"Is this... real?" I asked, incredulously.

"Yes, it's real," Mom said.

"Bruno!" Max shouted and looked around excitedly.

"Well, you'll have to look if you want to find Bruno," Dad said, and we started looking. We didn't care about the sweets. We just wanted to find Bruno. And we did! But not just Bruno, but nine more crickets with him! They were in a clear plastic box.

For the next few days and weeks we were allowed to keep Bruno, Supi, Stupsi, Pepsi, Cola, King, Rosti, Mix, Friedolin and Ruby. They lived in a terrarium with us in our room. We fed them every day and watched them every free minute. Time flew by.

I went to school again, Max to day care, and I had already gotten my new sandals when we were finally allowed to visit Grandma and Grandpa again. It was so great seeing them! And then we set the crickets free on the meadow in the garden. Pepsi and Cola hadn't make it, but the others scurried off in all directions. We rocked on the swing for hours, and on this day we were allowed to eat as much of Grandma's apple strudel as we wanted. Of course with vanilla ice cream. Meanwhile it chirped peacefully around us – and before us lay a wonderful summer.

The End

Dear children, dear reading public!

Did you like Bruno's story? If so, please recommend my book to other children - that's how Bruno makes his way around the world.

I would like to take this opportunity to thank my husband, Stine and her husband, my father, my sisters, Annabelle and Max, my closest friends, my anonymous readership on Instagram and also my translater, who worked for free to support the book.

Juni 2020